TEAM SPIRIT ®

SMART BOOKS FOR YOUNG FANS

THE INDIANA PACERS

BY
MARK STEWART

NORWOODHOUSE PRESS
CHICAGO, ILLINOIS

Norwood House Press
P.O. Box 316598
Chicago, Illinois 60631

For information regarding Norwood House Press, please visit our website at:
www.norwoodhousepress.com or call 866-565-2900.

All photos courtesy of Associated Press except the following:
Topps, Inc. (7, 15, 18, 21, 23, 27, 38, 43 right), Author's Collection (11, 28), Black Book Partners (26),
Indiana Pacers (33, 34, 42 top), JBC/NBA Hoops (35 left), Women Sport Magazine (36),
Fleer Corp. (42 bottom), The Star Company (45).
Cover Photo: Darron Cummings/Associated Press

The memorabilia and artifacts pictured in this book are presented for educational and informational purposes,
and come from the collection of the author.

Editor: Mike Kennedy
Designer: Ron Jaffe
Project Management: Black Book Partners, LLC.
Special thanks to Topps, Inc.

Library of Congress Cataloging-in-Publication Data

Stewart, Mark, 1960 July 7-
  The Indiana Pacers / by Mark Stewart.
    pages cm. -- (Team spirit)
  Includes bibliographical references and index.
  Summary: "A revised Team Spirit Basketball edition featuring the Indiana
Pacers that chronicles the history and accomplishments of the team. Includes
access to the Team Spirit website which provides additional information and
photos"-- Provided by publisher.
    ISBN 978-1-59953-634-7 (library edition : alk. paper) -- ISBN
978-1-60357-643-7 (ebook) 1. Indiana Pacers (Basketball
team)--History--Juvenile literature. I. Title.
  GV885.52.I53S74 2014
  796.323'640977252--dc23
                                        2014006550

253—072014
Manufactured in the United States of America in North Mankato, Minnesota.

COVER PHOTO: There is an endless amount of team spirit in Indiana for the Pacers.

Table of Contents

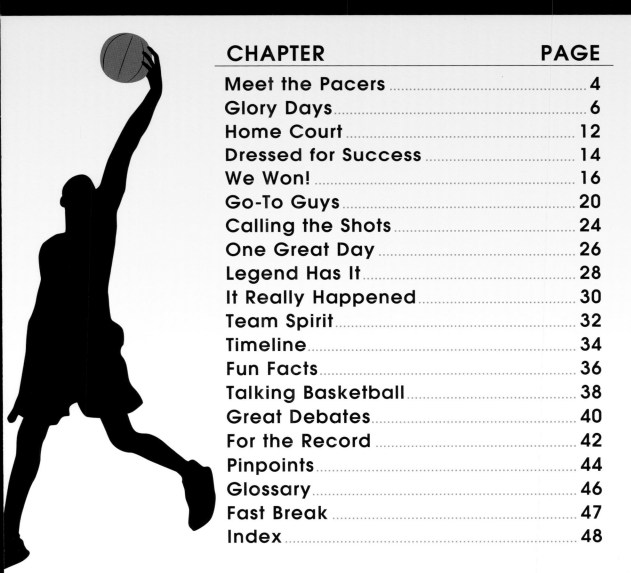

ABOUT OUR GLOSSARY

In this book, there may be several words that you are reading for the first time. Some are sports words, some are new vocabulary words, and some are familiar words that are used in an unusual way. All of these words are defined on page 46. Throughout the book, sports words appear in **bold type**. Regular vocabulary words appear in ***bold italic type***.

Meet the Pacers

There are many ways to win a basketball game. Some teams like to strike quickly and force an opponent to catch up. Others prefer to wait patiently for the other team to make a mistake. The Indiana Pacers use their strength and *stamina* to wear down their opponents, and then seize victory as the last minutes tick away.

The Pacers play in a region of the country where basketball is the most popular sport. Like football in Texas and hockey in Canada, basketball in Indiana is more than just a game. When the Pacers take the court, they know that they are upholding a great *tradition*.

This book tells the story of the Pacers. They keep games close by playing rugged defense and controlling the area around the basket. They win games with amazing individual efforts, often as the final buzzer sounds.

Roy Hibbert embraces Luis Scola during an Indiana victory in 2013–14.

Glory Days

To many in Indiana, basketball is like a religion. The state's gyms and arenas are like houses of worship. A basketball hero in Indiana is a hero for life. For the first half the 1900s, high school and college hoops ruled. In the 1940s and 1950s, several *professional* teams played in Indianapolis. However, the first to win over college and high school fans was the Indiana Pacers of the **American Basketball Association (ABA)**. They were one of 11 teams that helped form the new league in 1967.

The first player to make a name for himself with the Pacers was Roger Brown, a legendary one-on-one star from the playgrounds of New York City. Freddie Lewis joined him in the backcourt. He had an excellent all-around game and was a favorite of fans and teammates. It became a tradition that Lewis would take the first shot of every game. Over the next few years, the Pacers added other talented stars, including Bob Netolicky, Billy Keller, Rick Mount, and George McGinnis.

Indiana became a powerhouse, winning the ABA championship in 1970, 1972, and 1973. Bob "Slick" Leonard coached these teams. Leonard was an Indiana basketball legend himself. In 1953, he scored the winning points for Indiana University in the college basketball national championship.

MEL DANIELS
PACERS' CENTER

Indiana's top star during its ABA years was center Mel Daniels. Though he stood only 6' 9", no one was better near the basket. Daniels won the ABA's **Most Valuable Player (MVP)** award twice and was also the MVP of the ABA **All-Star Game**. He was a great defensive player and rebounder; no one in ABA history hauled down more rebounds.

Prior to the 1976–77 season, the **National Basketball Association (NBA)** invited four ABA teams to join the league, including the Pacers. After trading away many of its best players, Indiana tried to

LEFT: "Slick" Leonard was a huge favorite among Indiana fans.
ABOVE: Mel Daniels led the Pacers to three ABA titles.

rebuild around new leaders Don Buse and Billy Knight. Later, Indiana traded Buse and Knight away, too. For many years after that, the team struggled.

During the 1980s, the Pacers lost far more often than they won. Their best players were Herb Williams, Clark Kellogg, Steve Stipanovich, Wayman Tisdale, and Vern Fleming. As the *decade* came to a close, Indiana began to show signs of life. The Pacers benefitted greatly from three smart picks in the first round of the NBA **draft**. Chuck Person and Reggie Miller developed into remarkable shooters, and Rik Smits was an agile 7' 4" center.

During the 1990s, the Pacers missed the **playoffs** only once. Miller became one of the NBA's most amazing **clutch** players. Time and again, he made long shots before the final buzzer that either

LEFT: Reggie Miller celebrates a victory.
ABOVE: Chuck Person drives to the hoop for a layup.

tied games or won them. Rugged forwards Dale Davis and Antonio Davis gave the team good rebounding and defense. Guard Mark Jackson was one of the league's best floor leaders.

In 1997–98, Larry Bird became the team's coach. He was as big a basketball legend as Indiana had ever produced. With the help of role players such as Jalen Rose, Austin Croshere, and Travis Best, Bird led the club all the way to the 2000 **NBA Finals**. The Pacers played well against the Los Angeles Lakers, but they lost in six games.

The key moment came in Game 4. The Lakers won in **overtime** when Miller missed the winning shot. It was one of the few times in his career that he did not come through in the clutch.

Following their near-miss in 2000, the Pacers rebuilt around a new group of young players. In 2003–04, Indiana won 61 games—the most in team history. Miller retired a year later, allowing Jermaine O'Neal, Danny Granger, Jamaal Tinsley, and Roy Hibbert to step up and take leadership roles.

After so many years of success, Indiana fans were startled when their team went six seasons in a row without a winning record. Slowly but surely, the Pacers rebuilt their squad. With Hibbert, Granger, Luis Scola, and David West providing experienced leadership for newcomers Paul George, Lance Stephenson, and George Hill, the team quickly became one of the NBA's best. In 2013–14, Indiana finished with the best record in the **Eastern Conference**.

LEFT: Larry Bird gives instructions to Jalen Rose. **ABOVE**: Paul George signed this photo. He became a team leader in 2013–14.

The Pacers' first home court was the Indiana State Fair Coliseum. In 1974, the team moved into Market Square Arena. In 2008, the Pacers returned to the Coliseum for an exhibition game and wore their old uniforms from the 1960s.

In 1999, the Pacers moved into a beautiful new arena shaped like an old fieldhouse. Since then, many sports stadiums have copied this idea of mixing old-time style with modern *architecture*. Indiana fans love the team's arena. Many grew up in towns where the fieldhouse—with its curved roof and brick exterior—was the center of sports and social activity.

BY THE NUMBERS

- The Pacers' arena has 18,165 seats for basketball.

- As of 2013–14, the Pacers had retired four numbers—30 (George McGinnis), 31 (Reggie Miller), 34 (Mel Daniels), and 35 (Roger Brown).

- Jersey number 529 also hangs from the rafters in the arena. It is the number of games won by coach Slick Leonard.

The Pacers' arena feels like home to Indiana fans. Many learned how to play basketball in their town's fieldhouse.

Dressed for Success

The Pacers have used blue, white, and yellow as their colors since their first season. In recent years, they have made black a fourth color. Beginning in the 1980s, the Pacers started experimenting with different shades of blue. They also wore uniforms that included diagonal blocks of color. In 1998–99, Indiana introduced a fun *pinstripe* design.

The team's *logo* has always featured a *P* for Pacers. In Indiana's early years, it was formed by a player's outstretched arm grasping a basketball. The team used this logo until the 1990s, when it switched to a *P* surrounding a basketball. For their 40th anniversary, the Pacers unveiled a logo that included a picture of the state of Indiana, with a banner reading *1967–2007*.

LEFT: Lance Stephenson peeks at the scoreboard wearing the team's 2013–14 home uniform.   **ABOVE**: This trading card shows Roger Brown in the Pacers' road uniform of the early 1970s.

The first two champions of the ABA were built around a pair of superstars, Connie Hawkins and Rick Barry. Hawkins led the Pittsburgh Pipers to the 1968 title, and Barry was the leader of the Oakland Oaks a year later. But the 1970 ABA champions were a much different kind of team. The Pacers had a balanced roster and played unselfish basketball for a brilliant coach.

Indiana won 59 games in 1969–70 and had the ABA's best defense. The Pacers could score, too. Forwards Roger Brown and Bob Netolicky averaged more than 20 points a game, Mel Daniels was one of the league's best rebounders, and Freddie Lewis and John Barnhill were excellent outside shooters. In one game against the Pipers, Indiana scored 177 points!

In the 1970 playoffs, the Pacers easily defeated the Carolina Cougars in the first round. Next, they dismantled the Kentucky Colonels. In the **ABA Finals**, Indiana faced the Los Angeles Stars, who were known for their great rebounding. Daniels was up for the challenge. He outmuscled Los Angeles under the backboards, while

Mel Daniels swoops in for a layup against the Colonels.

Brown scored at will against the Stars' best defensive players. The Pacers won the series in six games to claim their first ABA crown.

Indiana returned to the ABA Finals in 1972. The Pacers were stronger than ever. George McGinnis, Rick Mount, Darnell Hillman, Larry Cannon, and Billy Keller joined the team to give the Pacers great depth. In the playoffs, they met the Denver Rockets. The teams split the first six games to set up a dramatic seventh game. The Pacers won in a tense battle, 91–89. They faced a rematch in the next round with the Stars (now in Utah). Again, the

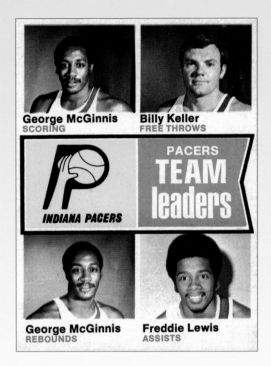

George McGinnis
SCORING

Billy Keller
FREE THROWS

PACERS TEAM leaders

INDIANA PACERS

George McGinnis
REBOUNDS

Freddie Lewis
ASSISTS

series went seven games. Indiana moved on with a 117–113 victory.

In the ABA Finals against the New York Nets, the Pacers got a championship effort from Lewis. He played great defense, set up teammates for easy shots, and scored one important basket after another. Thanks to his amazing performance, the Pacers won their second championship.

Indiana's final ABA championship came one year later. Daniels, Brown, and Lewis were still the heart of the team, but McGinnis was now the star. The big power forward averaged more than 27 points and 12 rebounds a game during the season. Coach Slick Leonard had talent up and down the roster. On any given night, eight different Pacers were capable of scoring in double-figures.

In the playoffs, Indiana took a familiar path to the championship round. The Pacers beat Denver and then Utah to set up a showdown with Kentucky for the ABA title. The Colonels had two of the league's best players, Artis Gilmore and Dan Issel. Indiana held its own, fighting for every loose ball and rebound. After six games, the series was tied.

Game 7 was played in Kentucky. It was 48 minutes of rough, tough basketball. When Daniels got into foul trouble, Leonard took a gamble and brought old-timer Gus Johnson into the game. Though nine inches shorter than Gilmore, he did a great job on the gigantic center. McGinnis poured in 27 points, and the Pacers won 88–81 for their third championship.

LEFT: This trading card shows three Pacers—George McGinnis, Billy Keller, and Freddie Lewis—who played a huge role in the team's last two ABA titles.
ABOVE: McGinnis was one of Slick Leonard's favorite players to coach.

To be a true star in the NBA, you need more than a great shot. You have to be a "go-to guy"—someone teammates trust to make the winning play when the seconds are ticking away in a big game. Pacers fans have had a lot to cheer about over the years, including these great stars ...

THE PIONEERS

ROGER BROWN   6′ 5″ Guard/Forward

• BORN: 5/22/1942   • DIED: 3/4/1997   • PLAYED FOR TEAM: 1967–68 TO 1974–75

No one in the ABA was harder to defend than Roger Brown. He was a great leaper and an excellent shooter. In Indiana's first ABA championship run, Brown averaged more than 28 points per game.

FREDDIE LEWIS   6′ 0″ Guard

• BORN: 7/1/1943   • PLAYED FOR TEAM: 1967–68 TO 1973–74 & 1976–77

Freddie Lewis formed one of the ABA's best backcourts with Roger Brown. Lewis always hustled and played like a superstar when it mattered most. He was named the MVP of the 1975 ABA All-Star Game.

MEL DANIELS   6′ 9″ Center

- BORN: 7/20/1944   • PLAYED FOR TEAM: 1968–69 TO 1973–74

Mel Daniels was strong, quick, and aggressive—and impossible to keep away from the basket. He was the top rebounder in ABA history, averaging more than 15 rebounds a game. Daniels was named ABA **Rookie of the Year** in 1968 and the MVP of the league twice.

GEORGE McGINNIS   6′ 8″ Forward

- BORN: 8/12/1950
- PLAYED FOR TEAM: 1971–72 TO 1974–75 & 1980–81 TO 1981–82

George McGinnis grew up in Indiana. Playing for the Pacers was a dream come true. He used his powerful body and one-handed jump shot to lead the ABA in scoring in 1974–75.

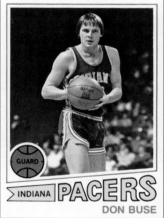

DON BUSE   6′ 4″ Guard

- BORN: 8/10/1950
- PLAYED FOR TEAM: 1972–73 TO 1976–77 & 1980–81 TO 1981–82

Don Buse was a good ball handler and an excellent defender. He was an All-Star in the ABA and later in the NBA. Buse led both leagues in steals and **assists**.

BILLY KNIGHT   6′ 6″ Guard/Forward

- BORN: 6/9/1952
- PLAYED FOR TEAM: 1974–75 TO 1976–77 & 1978–79 TO 1982–83

Billy Knight was a guard in a forward's body. He kept opponents off balance with his quickness. Knight retired as Indiana's all-time leading scorer.

ABOVE: Don Buse

CHUCK PERSON
6′ 8″ Forward

• BORN: 6/27/1964   • PLAYED FOR TEAM: 1986–87 TO 1991–92

Chuck Person brought the Pacers a much-needed spark in the 1980s. He took every game personally, which made his teammates try even harder to win. Person's nickname was the "Rifleman" because of his great outside shot.

REGGIE MILLER
6′ 7″ Guard

• BORN: 8/24/1965   • PLAYED FOR TEAM: 1987–88 TO 2004–05

No Indiana player was more intense than Reggie Miller. The Pacers played hard and talked tough during the 1990s, and Miller was their leader. When one shot meant the difference between victory and defeat, Indiana wanted the ball in his hands.

RIK SMITS
7′ 4″ Center

• BORN: 8/23/1966

• PLAYED FOR TEAM: 1988–89 TO 1999–2000

Rik Smits was nicknamed the "Dunking Dutchman." He was a dangerous outside shooter and tough around the hoop. Smits was at his best in the playoffs, when he battled the top centers in the Eastern Conference.

JERMAINE O'NEAL   6´ 11˝ Forward/Center

- BORN: 10/13/1978
- PLAYED FOR TEAM 2001–01 TO 2007–08

Jermaine O'Neal grew up playing guard, until he sprouted to nearly seven feet tall. He never stopped working on his game and became one of the NBA's best forwards. He made the All-Star team six years in a row with the Pacers.

ROY HIBBERT   7´ 2˝ Center

- BORN: 12/11/1986
- FIRST SEASON WITH TEAM: 2008–09

When the Pacers traded for Roy Hibbert, they saw great *potential* in him. Hibbert developed into a *dominant* defender and showed a special talent for grabbing offensive rebounds. By 2013–14, he was one of the best defensive players in the NBA.

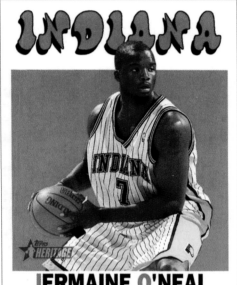

JERMAINE O'NEAL
PACERS' FORWARD-CENTER

PAUL GEORGE   6´ 9˝ Guard/Forward

- BORN: 5/2/1990   • FIRST SEASON WITH TEAM: 2010–11

The moment Paul George broke into the Indiana starting lineup in 2011, the comparisons to Reggie Miller began. George loved to shoot **3-pointers**, even with defenders right in his face. He also brought the crowd to its feet with amazing dunks.

LEFT: Rik Smits   **ABOVE**: Jermaine O'Neal

Calling the Shots

The Pacers made it to the playoffs in each of their nine ABA seasons. Their coach in eight of those seasons was Bob Leonard. In the 1950s, Leonard was a top guard whose smooth, clever play earned him the nickname "Slick." As a coach, Leonard led the Pacers to the ABA championship three times. He had a great relationship with his players—both the stars and the substitutes. They gave him lots of credit for their success.

Leonard continued to coach the Pacers for several years after they joined the NBA. Later, he became the team's television announcer. He was famous for yelling, "Boom baby!" when an Indiana player hit a 3-point shot.

In the 1980s, the Pacers had two excellent coaches, Jack McKinney and Jack Ramsay. McKinney was named NBA **Coach of the Year** in 1980–81. Ramsay had already won a championship when he arrived in Indianapolis and gave the Pacers a big boost of confidence.

During the 1990s, Larry Brown coached the Pacers. In 1994–95, he helped the team win its first **division** title since joining the NBA.

Larry Bird talks things over with Reggie Miller.

Brown guided the Pacers to the finals of the Eastern Conference in each of his first two seasons.

Larry Bird picked up where Brown left off. "Larry Legend" lived up to his nickname by winning two more division titles, and leading the club to the NBA Finals in 2000. Players of Bird's skill usually don't make good coaches. But Bird turned out to be as good a leader on the sidelines as he had been on the court. In the years that followed, Indiana returned to the playoffs under Isiah Thomas, Rick Carlisle, and Frank Vogel. In 2013, Vogel guided the Pacers to within one win of their second trip to the NBA Finals.

One Great Day

During a six-season stretch in the 1990s, the Pacers reached the Eastern Conference Finals four times. Each time, they

fell short of the NBA Finals. In 1999–2000, all that stood between the Pacers and the championship round was their old **rival**, the New York Knicks. Indiana took the first two games of the series, but the Knicks clawed back to tie it. Indiana won Game 5 at home and then traveled to New York hoping to close out the series.

The fans at Madison Square Garden roared after each New York basket, and booed Reggie Miller whenever he touched the ball. The Pacers built a 9-point lead at halftime, but then they went cold in the third quarter. They scored a mere 12 points—the lowest total ever for Indiana in a playoff game.

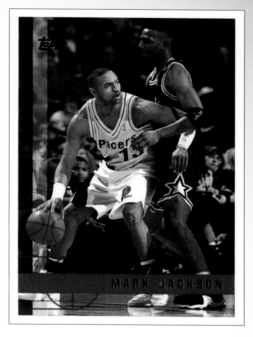

The Knicks fought back to take the lead late in the third quarter, 62–59. That's when Miller took over the game. He told coach Larry Bird and point guard Mark Jackson to run every play through him. He would either pass, shoot, or draw a foul. Miller hit a long 3-point shot to tie the score, and continued to burn the Knicks in the fourth quarter.

In the final 12 minutes, Miller hit three more 3-pointers and made eight free throws for a total of 17 points. He finished with 34 points, and Indiana won 93–80. When the final buzzer sounded, Miller hugged Dale Davis, who ruled the boards with 16 rebounds. Then he jumped into the arms of Jalen Rose. After so many near misses, the Pacers were finally on their way to the NBA Finals.

LEFT: Reggie Miller's performance in Game 6 of the 2000 Eastern Conference Finals was one of his best ever. **ABOVE**: Mark Jackson was smart to listen to Miller's advice in the second half of Game 6.

Legend Has It

DARNELL HILLMAN ▪ F

Who had basketball's biggest hair?

LEGEND HAS IT that Darnell Hillman did. During the 1970s, many players wore their hair in large Afros. Hillman's measured more than two feet from side to side. He stood 6' 9", but with his hair freshly styled, he measured well over seven feet tall. In 1997, a group of former ABA players gathered for a reunion. Hillman was given the Biggest ABA Afro Award.

ABOVE: Darnell Hillman shows off the hairdo that helped him win the Biggest ABA Afro Award.

Who was the Pacers' most popular player?

LEGEND HAS IT that Roger Brown was. Brown won over the fans in Indiana with great scoring and tough defense during his eight seasons with the Pacers. He helped the team win three ABA championships. The city's fans cheered for him off the court as well. In fact, Brown was so beloved and respected that the people of Indianapolis voted him to the City Council in 1971—while he was still a player!

Which Pacer once coached Larry Bird?

LEGEND HAS IT that Mel Daniels did. After his playing days with the Pacers, Daniels took a job as an assistant with Indiana State University. Larry Bird was the school's star player. Daniels worked with Bird on his defense and rebounding skills. Many years later, the two got together again. This time, Bird coached the Pacers and Daniels was the team's **Director of Player Personnel**.

For almost 20 years, the fourth quarter of Indiana games was known as "Miller Time." That is when Reggie Miller took over and turned from a great player into a legendary one. Miller's favorite team to beat was the New York Knicks, especially during the playoffs. He once scored eight points in the final nine seconds to hand New York a devastating loss.

However, Miller's most amazing performance came in Game 5 of the 1993–94 Eastern Conference Finals. The Knicks had a 70–58 lead when the final period began. The New York fans rose to their feet. They knew that the Pacers had lost their last 11 games on the Knicks' court, and were already counting number 12.

Early in the series, Miller was not playing with his usual fire. His teammates noticed this and pleaded with him to find that intensity. As Game 5 started, Miller was back in a groove. He scored 14 points in the first three quarters, but his best was yet to come. Miller made seven of his first eight shots in the fourth quarter, including five 3-pointers. He also scored on several amazing drives to the hoop.

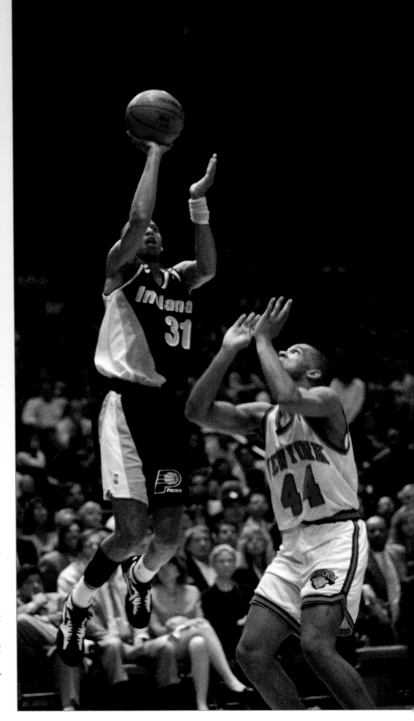

Reggie Miller rises for a shot during Game 5 of the 1994 Eastern Conference Finals.

After a long jump shot by Miller, the Pacers took the lead. As he ran down the court, Miller turned to the New York crowd and let the fans know that the Pacers would not lose. Indiana went on to a 93–86 victory.

Miller poured in 39 points, including 25 in the fourth quarter. "I felt as if everything was in slow motion," he said afterward, "like I was lifted above the court and I could see plays before they actually happened ... it was weird!"

The Pacers and their fans have had a special bond that dates back to the 1960s. Anyone who has played for Indiana is treated like an old friend when he returns to Indianapolis. When former Pacers visit the team's arena, the fans rise and cheer when their names are announced.

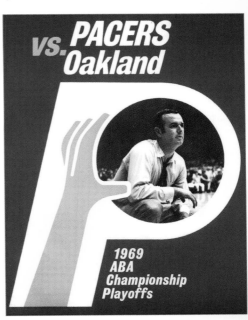

When the Pacers joined the NBA in 1977, they had to sell 8,000 season tickets to afford the league's entry fee. The head of a local television station held a telethon until enough tickets were sold. Today, the Pacers are still saying thanks to their fans. During games, the Pacemates dance team performs with the Junior Pacemates and the Hip-Hop Hoopsters. The Pacers also have a fun mascot. His name is Boomer, and he's a slam-dunking cat.

LEFT: Boomer is a fan favorite in Indianapolis.   **ABOVE**: Pacers fans bought this program during the 1969 ABA playoffs.

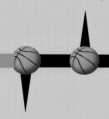The basketball season is played from October through June. That means each season takes place at the end of one year and the beginning of the next. In this timeline, the accomplishments of the Pacers are shown by season.

1969–70
The Pacers win their first ABA championship.

1974–75
George McGinnis leads the ABA in scoring.

1967–68
The Pacers play their first season.

1972–73
Indiana wins its third ABA championship.

1976–77
The Pacers join the NBA.

The ABA champions show off their warm-ups in this 1973 team picture.

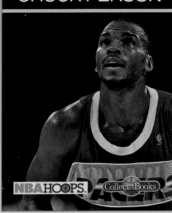

CHUCK PERSON

Chuck
Person

Larry
Bird

1986–87
Chuck Person is named
Rookie of the Year.

1997–98
Larry Bird is named
Coach of the Year.

2003–04
Indiana leads the
NBA with 61 wins.

1996–97
Mark Jackson leads
the NBA in assists.

1999–2000
The Pacers reach the NBA
Finals for the first time.

2012–13
Roy Hibbert sets a
team record with
11 blocks in a game.

Roy Hibbert
makes one of
his 11 blocks.

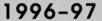

Fun Facts

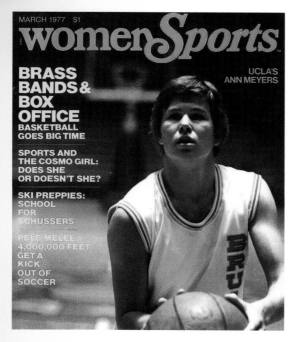

MARCH 1977 $1
women Sports
BRASS
BANDS &
BOX
OFFICE
BASKETBALL
GOES BIG TIME

SPORTS AND
THE COSMO GIRL:
DOES SHE
OR DOESN'T SHE?

SKI PREPPIES:
SCHOOL
FOR
SCHUSSERS

PELE MELEE:
4,000,000 FEET
GET A
KICK
OUT OF
SOCCER

UCLA'S
ANN MEYERS

WONDER WOMAN

In 1979, the Pacers signed college star Ann Meyers to a $50,000 contract. Although Meyers didn't make the team, she worked on Indiana's television broadcasts that season.

STUPID GOOD

When Indiana coach Frank Vogel was an eighth grader, he appeared on *Late Night with David Letterman.* He brushed his teeth while spinning a basketball on the end of the toothbrush as part of "Stupid Human Tricks."

GETTING DEFENSIVE

Paul George was a player best known for his scoring ability. However, in 2012–13, George was the only NBA player with at least 140 steals and 50 blocked shots.

SWEET MUSIC

Wayman Tisdale starred for Indiana in the 1980s. He was also a jazz musician. His first album was named *Power Forward*—the position he played during his NBA days.

DOUBLE TEAM

In 2007, Roy Hibbert played center for Team USA at the **Pan American Games**. In 2010, Hibbert was named captain of the Jamaican national team. Although he was born in New York, Hibbert's parents are Jamaican, so he was allowed to play for that country in *international* tournaments.

SWISH CITY

The Pacers are the third NBA team to play in Indianapolis. The city was home to the Jets for one season in the 1940s and the Olympians for four seasons in the early 1950s.

LEFT: Ann Meyers   **ABOVE**: Wayman Tisdale

Talking Basketball

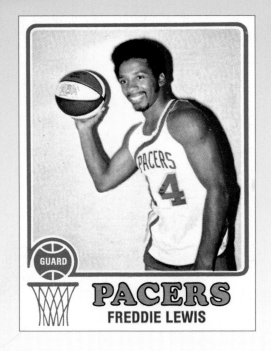

GUARD

PACERS
FREDDIE LEWIS

"This is where I played the majority of my career. This is my team."

▶ **Freddie Lewis,** *on the pride of being a Pacer*

"Nothing comes easy. You have to work for everything."

▶ **Roy Hibbert,** *on what it takes to be an All-Star*

"For six or seven years, we were really the best. We had this attitude: *Who's going to beat us?* A few little tweaks and we could have won five titles in a row."

▶ **Bob Netolicky,** *on the Pacers of the early 1970s*

"I think blocking a shot at a crucial point of the game is the most incredible feeling."

▶ **Jermaine O'Neal,** *on making game-changing plays*

"I always wanted the ball in my hands if it was ever close and the game was on the line."

► **Reggie Miller,** *on what made him a great clutch player*

"I don't say this lightly. Roger Brown was phenomenal."

► **Mel Daniels,** *on his superstar teammate*

"The only way for me to get on the court in the NBA was to play defense, so that was something I had to hang my hat on."

► **Paul George,** *on why he worked so hard to become a good defender*

"If anybody could get a team up for a game, it was Slick. He was crazy."

► **Roger Brown,** *on coach Slick Leonard*

LEFT: Freddie Lewis   **ABOVE**: Reggie Miller

Great Debates

People who root for the Pacers love to compare their favorite moments, teams, and players. Some debates have been going on for years! How would you settle these classic basketball arguments?

Jermaine O'Neal was the Pacers' finest power forward ...

... because he combined rugged defense with explosive scoring. When O'Neal (**LEFT**) was healthy, there wasn't a better power forward in the NBA. He was a six-time All-Star and a member of the **All-NBA Team** three times. O'Neal came to the Pacers when three beloved stars—Mark Jackson, Rik Smits, and Chris Mullin—were leaving the team. He went on to average 20 or more points four seasons in a row.

Go ahead and put George McGinnis ahead of O'Neal ...

... because McGinnis was a monster. He could score at will, and used his quick hands and big body to make great defensive plays. McGinnis was a key member of three championship teams, he led the ABA in scoring, and was co-MVP the same year that Julius Erving was the league scoring champ. That tells you just how good McGinnis was!

Paul George's dunk at the 2012 All-Star Game was the most amazing in team history ...

... because he jumped over two teammates to do it. Dahntay Jones and Roy Hibbert lined up between the free throw line and the basket. George (RIGHT) dribbled toward them, jumped over Hibbert's head, cleared Jones's head, and then jammed the ball in the basket.

That shot was made during the Slam Dunk Contest. Jerry Harkness's 92-foot shot in 1967–68 was more amazing ...

... because he made it during an actual game. Harkness flung the ball from under his own basket with the Pacers behind by two points. He had no choice—there was just one second left in the game. It was the first season of the ABA, and people were still getting used to the 3-pointer. When Harkness's shot went in, both teams went to the bench to get ready for overtime. The referee had to tell the Pacers that they had won the game, 119–118!

The great Pacers teams and players have left their marks on the record books. These are the "best of the best" …

Larry Bird

Ron Artest

PACERS AWARD WINNERS

ABA MVP

Mel Daniels	1968–69
Mel Daniels	1970–71
George McGinnis	1974–75*

ABA FINALS MVP

Roger Brown	1969–70
Freddie Lewis	1971–72
George McGinnis	1972–73

ABA SLAM DUNK CHAMPION

Mel Daniels	1970–71

NBA MOST IMPROVED PLAYER

Jalen Rose	1999–00
Jermaine O'Neal	2001–02
Danny Granger	2008–09
Paul George	2012–13

NBA SIXTH MAN AWARD

Detlef Schrempf	1990–91
Detlef Schrempf	1991–92

NBA ROOKIE OF THE YEAR

Chuck Person	1986–87

NBA SLAM DUNK CHAMPION

Fred Jones	2003–04

NBA COACH OF THE YEAR

Jack McKinney	1980–81
Larry Bird	1997–98

NBA DEFENSIVE PLAYER OF THE YEAR

Ron Artest	2003–04

* Shared award with another player.

PACERS ACHIEVEMENTS

ACHIEVEMENT	SEASON
ABA Eastern Division Champions	1968–69
ABA Eastern Division Champions	1969–70
ABA Champions	1969–70
ABA Western Division Champions	1970–71
ABA Champions	1971–72
ABA Champions	1972–73
NBA Central Division Champions	1994–95
NBA Central Division Champions	1998–99
NBA Central Division Champions	1999–00
NBA Eastern Conference Champions	1999–00
NBA Central Division Champions	2003–04
NBA Central Division Champions	2013–14

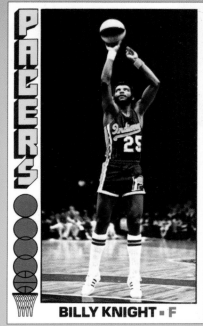

BILLY KNIGHT ▪ F

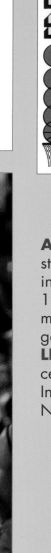

ABOVE: Billy Knight starred for the Pacers in the 1970s and 1980s. He averaged more than 18 points a game with Indiana.
LEFT: Austin Croshere celebrates during Indiana's run to the NBA Finals in 2000.

43

Pinpoints

The history of a basketball team is made up of many smaller stories. These stories take place all over the map—not just in the city a team calls "home." Match the pushpins on these maps to the **TEAM FACTS**, and you will begin to see the story of the Pacers unfold!

TEAM FACTS

1 Indianapolis, Indiana—*The Pacers have played here since 1967.*
2 Detroit, Michigan—*Mel Daniels was born here.*
3 St. Louis, Missouri—*Steve Stipanovich was born here.*
4 Braddock, Pennsylvania—*Billy Knight was born here.*
5 Brooklyn, New York—*Roger Brown was born here.*
6 Columbia, South Carolina—*Jermaine O'Neal was born here.*
7 Toccoa, Georgia—*Dale Davis was born here.*
8 Brantley, Alabama—*Chuck Person was born here.*
9 Tulsa, Oklahoma—*Wayman Tisdale was born here.*
10 Palmdale, California—*Paul George was born here.*
11 Eindhoven, Netherlands—*Rik Smits was born here.*
12 Buenos Aires, Argentina—*Luis Scola was born here.*

Steve Stipanovich

Glossary

🗣 **3-POINTERS**—Shots attempted from behind the 3-point line.

🗣 **ABA FINALS**—The series that decided the ABA champion.

🗣 **ALL-NBA TEAM**—The annual honor given to the NBA's best players at each position.

🗣 **ALL-STAR GAME**—The annual game in which the league's best players play against each other. The game does not count in the standings.

🗣 **AMERICAN BASKETBALL ASSOCIATION (ABA)**—The basketball league that played for nine seasons starting in 1967.

🧠 *ARCHITECTURE*—A style of building.

🗣 **ASSISTS**—Passes that lead to baskets.

🗣 **CLUTCH**—Able to perform well under pressure.

🗣 **COACH OF THE YEAR**—The annual award given to the league's best coach.

🧠 *DECADE*—A period of 10 years; also specific periods, such as the 1950s.

🗣 **DIRECTOR OF PLAYER PERSONNEL**—The person in charge of building a team's roster.

🗣 **DIVISION**—A group of teams within a league that play in the same part of the country.

🧠 *DOMINANT*—Ruling or controlling.

🗣 **DRAFT**—The annual meeting during which NBA teams choose from a group of the best college players.

🗣 **EASTERN CONFERENCE**—A group of teams that play in the East. The winner of the Eastern Conference meets the winner of the Western Conference in the league finals.

🧠 *INTERNATIONAL*—From all over the world.

🧠 *LOGO*—A symbol or design that represents a company or team.

🗣 **MOST VALUABLE PLAYER (MVP)**—The annual award given to the league's best player; also given to the best player in the league finals and All-Star Game.

🗣 **NATIONAL BASKETBALL ASSOCIATION (NBA)**—The professional league that has been operating since 1946–47.

🗣 **NBA FINALS**—The playoff series that decides the champion of the league.

🗣 **OVERTIME**—The extra period played when a game is tied after 48 minutes.

🗣 **PAN AMERICAN GAMES**—An international sports competition held every four years.

🗣 **PLAYOFFS**—The games played after the season to determine the league champion.

🧠 *PINSTRIPE*—A style with thin stripes.

🧠 *POTENTIAL*—The ability to become better.

🧠 *PROFESSIONAL*—A player or team that plays a sport for money.

🧠 *RIVAL*— Extremely emotional competitor.

🗣 **ROOKIE OF THE YEAR**—The annual award given to the league's best first-year player.

🧠 *STAMINA*—The ability to sustain a long physical effort.

🧠 *TRADITION*—A belief or custom that is handed down from generation to generation.

FAST BREAK

TEAM SPIRIT introduces a great way to stay up to date with your team! Visit our **FAST BREAK** link and get connected to the latest and greatest updates. **FAST BREAK** serves as a young reader's ticket to an exclusive web page—with more stories, fun facts, team records, and photos of the Pacers. Content is updated during and after each season. The **FAST BREAK** feature also enables readers to send comments and letters to the author! Log onto:

www.norwoodhousepress.com/library.aspx

and click on the tab: **TEAM SPIRIT** to access **FAST BREAK**.

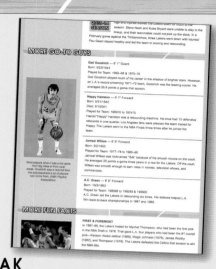

Read all the books in the series to learn more about professional sports. For a complete listing of the baseball, basketball, football, and hockey teams in the **TEAM SPIRIT** series, visit our website at:

www.norwoodhousepress.com/library.aspx

On the Road

INDIANA PACERS
125 South Pennsylvania Street
Indianapolis, Indiana 46204
(317) 917-2500
www.pacers.com

**NAISMITH MEMORIAL
BASKETBALL HALL OF FAME**
1000 West Columbus Avenue
Springfield, Massachusetts 01105
(877) 4HOOPLA
www.hoophall.com

On the Bookshelf

To learn more about the sport of basketball, look for these books at your library or bookstore:

• Doeden, Matt. *Basketball Legends In the Making*. North Mankato, Minnesota: Capstone Press, 2014.

• Rappaport, Ken. *Basketball's Top 10 Slam Dunkers*. Berkeley Heights, New Jersey: Enslow Publishers, 2013.

• Silverman, Drew. *The NBA Finals*. Minneapolis, Minnesota: ABDO Group, 2013.

Index

THE TEAM

MARK STEWART has written more than 40 books on basketball, and over 150 sports books for kids. He grew up in New York City during the 1960s rooting for the Knicks and Nets, and was lucky enough to meet many of the stars of those teams. Mark comes from a family of writers. His grandfather was Sunday Editor of *The New York Times* and his mother was Articles Editor of *The Ladies' Home Journal* and *McCall's*. Mark has profiled hundreds of athletes over the last 20 years. He has also written several books about his native New York, and New Jersey, his home today. Mark is a graduate of Duke University, with a degree in History. He lives with his daughters and wife Sarah overlooking Sandy Hook, New Jersey.